IMAGES OF

GERMAN SELF-PROPELLED ARTILLERY AT WAR 1940-1945

RARE PHOTOGRAPHS FROM WARTIME ARCHIVES

Ian Baxter

Pen & Sword
MILITARY

First published in Great Britain in 2023 by
PEN & SWORD MILITARY
an imprint of Pen & Sword Books Ltd
Yorkshire – Philadelphia

ISBN 978-1-39906-868-0

Typeset by Concept, Huddersfield, West Yorkshire, HD4 5JL.
Printed and bound in the UK on paper from a sustainable source by
CPI Group (UK) Ltd, Croydon, CR0 4YY.

Pen & Sword Books Limited incorporates the imprints of After the Battle Atlas, Archaeology, Aviation, Discovery, Family History, Fiction, History, Maritime, Military, Military Classics, Politics, Select, Transport, True Crime, Air World, Frontline Publishing, Leo Cooper, Remember When, Seaforth Publishing, The Praetorian Press, Wharncliffe Local History, Wharncliffe Transport, Wharncliffe True Crime and White Owl.

For a complete list of Pen & Sword titles please contact
PEN & SWORD BOOKS LTD
47 Church Street, Barnsley, South Yorkshire, S70 2AS, England
E-mail: enquiries@pen-and-sword.co.uk
Website: www.pen-and-sword.co.uk
or
PEN & SWORD BOOKS
1950 Lawrence Rd, Havertown, PA 19083, USA
E-mail: uspen-and-sword@casematepublishers.com
Website: www.penandswordbooks.com

Contents

About the Author

Ian Baxter is a military historian who specializes in German twentieth-century military history. He has written more than fifty books including *Poland – The Eighteen Day Victory March*, *Panzers In North Africa*, *The Ardennes Offensive*, *The Western Campaign*, *The 12th SS Panzer-Division Hitlerjugend*, *The Waffen-SS on the Western Front*, *The Waffen-SS on the Eastern Front*, *The Red Army at Stalingrad*, *Elite German Forces of World War II*, *Armoured Warfare*, *German Tanks of War*, *Blitzkrieg*, *Panzer-Divisions at War 1939–1945*, *Hitler's Panzers*, *German Armoured Vehicles of World War Two*, *Last Two Years of the Waffen-SS at War*, *German Soldier Uniforms and Insignia*, *German Guns of the Third Reich*, *Defeat to Retreat: The Last Years of the German Army At War 1943–45*, *Operation Bagration – the Destruction of Army Group Centre*, *German Guns of the Third Reich*, *Rommel and the Afrika Korps*, *U-Boat War*, and most recently *The Sixth Army and the Road to Stalingrad*. He has written over a hundred articles including 'Last days of Hitler', 'Wolf's Lair', 'The Story of the V1 and V2 Rocket Programme', 'Secret Aircraft of World War Two', 'Rommel at Tobruk', 'Hitler's War With his Generals', 'Secret British Plans to Assassinate Hitler', 'The SS at Arnhem', 'Hitlerjugend', 'Battle of Caen 1944', 'Gebirgsjäger at War', 'Panzer Crews', 'Hitlerjugend Guerrillas', 'Last Battles in the East', 'The Battle of Berlin', and many more. He has also reviewed numerous military studies for publication, supplied thousands of photographs and important documents to various publishers and film production companies world-wide, and lectures to various schools, colleges and universities throughout the United Kingdom and Southern Ireland.

Introduction

One of the main abilities of the German *Panzerwaffe* was its skill and rapid speed in engaging its foe with concentrated force. However, occasionally this was not enough and additional firepower was often required to break through enemy lines. While towed ordnance was capable of achieving success, it was soon considered that a more rapid suitable solution was required, such as utilizing and converting tanks into fast-moving self-propelled artillery vehicles. As a result a number of armoured vehicles were transformed throughout the war including the Pz.Kpfw.I and II into the 15cm sIG.33 infantry gun known as the 'Bison'. Other conversions followed including the Pz.Kpfw.II *Wespe* ('Wasp') with its 10.5cm gun. There was the Pz.Kpfw.III/IV *Hummel* that boasted a 15cm howitzer, the *Sturmpanzer Brummbär*, the *Grille* series based on the Czech Pz.Kpfw.38(t) tank chassis and then there was the most famous and durable self-propelled artillery in the German army, the *Wespe*. Most of these vehicles achieved notable success on the battlefield, providing close fire support for infantry and even in a number of roles acting as specialized anti-tank vehicles.

This book is a highly illustrated record of the role played by German self-propelled artillery, from its beginnings in 1940 in France to North Africa, Italy, Russia and North-West Europe. It analyses the development of these deadly machines and describes how the Germans carefully utilized all available resources and reserves into building numerous variants in order to support and sustain their infantry on the battlefield. It depicts how these formidable weapons were adapted and up-gunned to face the ever-increasing enemy threat. With rare and often previously unpublished photographs, this book provides a unique insight into German self-propelled artillery from its early triumphant days in 1940 to its demise in 1945.

Chapter One

1940–41

The German army's invasion of Poland in September 1939 had taken no more than eighteen days to achieve its objectives. By this time the Germans had, moreover, swept every Polish division clean off the map, brought their thundering Panzer divisions to the very far corners of eastern Poland and outflanked and outmanoeuvred their opponents with skill and tactical brilliance. Yet, in spite of the string of successes in Poland, the German invasion had shown that towed infantry guns assigned to the infantry gun companies of the motorized infantry regiments had countless problems in keeping pace with the Panzers during combat. Much of the German army was animal draught and as a result German armoured vehicles frequently outstripped their supporting artillery and became vulnerable to enemy fire. German strategists therefore sought to develop artillery that could provide close fire support for infantry and also act as specialized anti-tank vehicles.

In late 1939 designers began putting together plans for self-propelled artillery vehicles with which artillery guns could be mounted on the chassis of a tank or halftrack. In order to give these vehicles more flexibility on the battlefield and enhance their speed, they would be lightly-armoured. Although constructed insufficiently to withstand direct combat fire, the crews would be protected against shrapnel and small-arms fire by a splinter shield bolted to the chassis. It was considered that many of these self-propelled armoured fighting vehicles would be equipped with machine guns for defence against enemy infantry fire.

The Germans knew that the key to success on the battlefield would be in utilizing self-propelled artillery over towed artillery. This would ensure that artillery batteries could reach the front lines quickly and effectively without being left behind by the rapid advance of the Panzers. The invasion of Poland had clearly shown German tacticians in the field that moving artillery by animal draught was antiquated and slow. Prior to a fire mission towed artillery had to stop, unlimber and the crew had to go through the laborious process of setting up the gun. To move position, the gun had to be limbered up again and brought – mainly by horse – to a new location. This process was hardly the German blitzkrieg doctrine that had been formulated to win wars by using offensive warfare designed to strike a swift, focused blow at an enemy using mobile, manoeuvrable forces, including armoured tanks and air support. The only way that blitzkrieg could be achieved cohesively was to adopt self-propelled artillery in the field. Unlike towed artillery, these mounted artillery vehicles could move swiftly, stop quickly, choose a location and then begin firing almost immediately. They would then quickly move on to a new position. Their ability to fire and move would make mobile conflict particularly successful during an advance. The capabilities of self-propelled artillery also meant the increased survivability of the units fighting in the field. Mobility on the battlefield was key to the success of the self-propelled vehicles, but designers knew that success also depended on weight, speed, range and ability to move. The tactical requirements of self-propelled artillery emerged from the need to follow the Panzer into action over long distances. At a moment's notice the vehicle could halt, change direction and quickly fire at an enemy target. The German principle of attack was all about fast-moving and changing combat.

In preparation for operations against the West, the Germans began designing a self-propelled artillery weapon. The first prototype built by Altmärkische Kettenfabrik GmbH in Berlin began with developers securing an unmodified 15cm sIG.33 howitzer complete with steel wheels on top of the chassis of a turretless Pz.Kpfw.I *Ausf.*B variant Panzer. Trials commenced to determine weight distribution and speed of the tank including its versatility across terrain. In spite of suspension issues, designers then adapted the 15cm gun and installed it. While the chassis remained unaltered, the turret and superstructure were removed. An upper three-sided box-like super-structure was added. The rear part of the vehicle was open in order to provide the crew with room to work and be re-supplied with ammunition. During its trials designers found the vehicle satisfactory, in spite of some weight issues. Trials were completed by March 1940. In total thirty-eight vehicles were produced and they formed part of the *Schwere Infanteriegeschütz Kompanie sIG (mot.) Kp* ('self-propelled heavy infantry gun companies'). Six companies were formed consisting of six vehicles numbering 701 to 706. The remaining two vehicles were held back in reserve and were allocated to new crews for training.

Just prior to the invasion of the West, the sIG (mot.) Kp companies were attached to the *Schützen-Brigade* ('rifle brigade') of various Panzer divisions: the 701st to the 9th Panzer Division, the 702nd to the 1st Panzer Division, the 703rd to the 2nd Panzer Division, the 704th to the 5th Panzer Division, the 705th to the 7th Panzer Division and the 706th to the 10th Panzer Division. Each of these companies comprised a command unit equipped with four military support vehicles, as well as four motorcycles including one with a sidecar combination complete with an MG 34 for local defence. The companies were divided into three two-vehicle platoons, and were supported by four Sd.Kfz.10 half-tracks with two trailers and two motorcycles. Additional vehicles including reconnaissance were used together with a couple of trucks for ammunition, fuel and spare parts.

By the time the war against the West was launched in May 1940, the Germans had put together a huge arsenal of armoured vehicles. In total there were some 2,072 tanks comprising Pz.Kpfw.I (640), Pz.Kpfw.II (825), Pz.Kpfw.III (456), Pz.Kpfw.IV (366), Pz.Kpfw.35(t) (151) and Pz.Kpfw.38(t) (264). The reserves comprised some 160 vehicles to replace combat losses and 135 Pz.Kpfw.Is and Pz.Kpfw.IIs that had been converted into armoured command tanks, which resulted them losing their armament. All the vehicles were distributed among the ten Panzer divisions. In addition to the main armoured force that made up the powerful Panzer divisions, various other types of armoured units were used. There were, for instance, four independent *Sturmartillerie* batteries, each of six *Sturmgeschütz* (StuG) III assault guns. Supporting the armoured advance and distributed between six Panzer divisions were the sIG (mot.) Kp companies making their debut. These box-like vehicles captured the attention of many of the infantrymen and Panzer crews that saw them for the first time bucketing along the roads and across the fields.

However, it was not just self-propelled artillery that the Germans used in France; they also adapted tanks to carry anti-tank guns as well. These self-propelled anti-tank guns or *Panzerjäger* were Pz.Kpfw.I *Ausf.*B tanks equipped with 4.7cm PaK guns bolted to the top of the chassis. For the Battle of France there were five *Panzerjäger* companies equipped with a 4.7cm PaK *auf* Pz.Kpfw.I, which was known as the Marder I tank destroyer. The vehicle provided mobile anti-tank support for infantry divisions.

To support the blitzkrieg there was a single company of ten 8.8cm Flak 18 *auf Schwere Zugkraftwagens*. These 8.8cm Flak guns were also adapted and mounted on the chassis of an armoured Sd.Kfz.7 half-track in order to give much-needed firepower support against the thickly-armoured British Matilda and French Char B tanks.

Yet in spite of the recommendation for self-propelled artillery in the field, the bulk of the guns used for operations against the West were still pulled by animal draught as most of the towing vehicles were reserved for Panzer and motorized divisions. This left almost all the four 10.5cm leFH.18 guns and heavy battalions consisting of three batteries equipped with four 15cm sFH.18 heavy gun howitzers being towed by horses. However, in spite of the almost total reliance on animals towing ordnance, the invasion of the West, which concluded with the Battle of France, was a victory for the Germans. They had reaped the fruits of another dramatic blitzkrieg campaign. France had proven ideal tank country in which to undertake a lightning war and its conception seemed flawless. While the *sIG (mot.) Kp* only contributed a small part of the armoured triumph, self-propelled artillery had proved very effective. However, it was not without its issues. While firepower, mobility and general reliability seemed satisfactory, there were numerous mechanical breakdowns, especially with the transmission. The 703rd Company, for instance, noted that out of its six vehicles, by 17 May only one remained operational due to three of them developing mechanical issues and the remaining two lost to enemy fire. At the end of the battle the 706th Company outlined a performance report and noted the following:

> The sIG.33 *auf* Pz.Kpfw.I *Ausf.*B has not performed well. However, its gun, during action, was effective and exceeded our requirements. The Pz.Kpfw.I chassis was not very strong. The running gear, although overhauled at Alkett, was very worn out after a number of years in service. The major failures were (up to 60 per cent) with the clutches, brakes and the tracks. The majority of sIG companies could not keep pace with the marching speed of the tank division, which frequently exceeded 30 kph. Due to this major issue, we advise to attach the sIG companies to infantry divisions for future combat … Combat usually involved a single sIG.33 gun firing from a concealed position at ranges varying from 50 to 4,000m. However, the front gun shield was repeatedly penetrated by armour-piercing infantry ammunition.

Following operations on the Western Front more self-propelled artillery vehicles were built, but no change in design or firepower were thought to be required. Other than a slight change in the organizational structure of adding and enlarging radio equipment, and introducing a command unit with additional vehicles and radio equipment, self-propelled artillery companies remained more or less the same.

By April 1941 the sIG (mot.) companies comprising the 701st, 703rd and 704th were once again in action, this time fighting in Yugoslavia and later against weak Greek forces. The sIG.33 *auf* Pz.I was attached to the 2nd, 5th and 8th Panzer divisions, but saw limited operations and with insignificant losses. The only loss recorded was by the 703rd Company which lost all of its six vehicles following an accident. On 19 May 1941 the 703rd Company, in preparation for war against Russia, had been withdrawn following the successful campaign in the Balkans and shipped from Patras in Greece to Taranto in Italy. However, the vessel *Marburg* transporting the self-propelled vehicles hit a mine and sank, sending all the vehicles from the 703rd to the bottom of the sea. Although the company was not disbanded, it was re-equipped with towed 15cm sIG guns instead.

A month later the German war machine finally turned its might to the East and launched an invasion of the Soviet Union known as Operation BARBAROSSA. The German force of almost 3 million men was divided into a total of 105 infantry divisions and 32 Panzer divisions. There were 3,332 tanks, more than 7,000 artillery pieces, 60,000 motor vehicles and 625,000 horses. Among these were just thirty sIG.33 *auf* Pz.Is available for action. These self-propelled artillery vehicles were hardly a serious threat to the Russians, but German commanders did not expect there to be much resistance and the war would be won before winter anyway. As with the invasion of France and the Balkans, the independent self-propelled heavy infantry gun companies initially maintained the same assignment numbers of 701 to 706 operating with the same Panzer divisions. However, once again, animal draught was key to the movement of artillery through Russia during the summer of 1941. In fact, there were some 25,000 horses alone that were used to move guns and supplies. Although this type of transportation did not cause its commanders initial concern, in some areas the supply lines were overstretched, and artillery being towed by horse could not keep up with the fast-moving tracked vehicles. As a result parts of the front stagnated and fierce battles were fought against growing Russian resistance.

Although the self-propelled heavy infantry gun companies made little difference in the conduct of war on the Eastern Front, the vehicles performed well. This was coupled with the fact that the artillery *truppen* had been well-trained, both in operating the vehicles and rectifying any mechanical problems in the field. The design of the assault gun had also contributed to its success. The low trajectory of the gun meant that it could effectively attack and penetrate enemy bunker installations, artillery positions, machine-gun and mortar dugouts too. Being fully tracked, it could quickly move from one position to another and be used in a supporting role for infantry. Although the gun did not have suitable anti-tank capability, it was able to attack enemy armour with some degree of success. Its effective gun had a shot range of 4,700 metres and a rate of fire of two to three rounds per minute. Yet, in spite of their success, the vehicles remained heavy and cumbersome, especially during off-road combat. Luckily for their crews, the enemy they often confronted was still poorly-led and trained. However, Russia was vast and the distances over which these vehicles had to travel were immense. As a consequence, they often broke down. This was made worse when the autumn rains arrived in October 1941 and conditions began to change. Cold driving rain fell along the German front and within hours the Russian countryside had been turned into a quagmire, with roads and fields becoming virtually impassable. Many of the roads leading to the East had become boggy swamps. Although tanks and other tracked vehicles managed to push through the mire at a slow pace, animal draught, trucks and other wheeled vehicles became hopelessly stuck in deep mud. To make matters worse, during November the German supply lines became increasingly overstretched, their vehicles were breaking down and casualty returns were mounting. Stiff resistance also began to hinder progress. It was for this reason and the fact that the war would not end in 1941 that the Germans required more self-propelled artillery vehicles. Although the sIG.33 *auf* Pz.I self-propelled gun had solved mobility for fast-moving artillery units, by the autumn of 1941 the vehicle was regarded as inadequate. Designers and engineers were therefore planning more similar vehicles for the coming year. The 'Bison', although not the greatest weapon on the battlefield, had in fact influenced the future development of self-propelled artillery.

Three photographs showing the 15cm sFH.18 howitzer being towed on a gun carriage. One shows the gun during a training exercise and other two with it being hauled slowly by animal draught. The sFH.18 was one of Germany's three main 15cm-calibre weapons, the others being the 15cm Kanone 18, a corps-level heavy howitzer, and the 15cm sIG.33, which was a short-barrelled infantry gun.

(**Opposite, above**) During winter action and a battery of Waffen-SS can be seen here with their 15cm sIG.33 infantry guns. The gun was the largest infantry weapon in the German arsenal, but was very heavy and initially horse-drawn. As a consequence the weight meant that the gun could not safely be towed above 10mph, and this caused far-reaching problems for the batteries in keeping up with the fast-moving armour. While towed ordnance was capable of achieving success, it was decided following the Polish campaign in 1939 that a more rapid suitable solution was required such as utilizing and converting tanks into fast-moving self-propelled artillery vehicles. As a result a number of armoured vehicles were transformed, including the Pz.Kpfw.I and II into the 15cm sIG.33 infantry gun.

(**Opposite, below**) Seen here parked in a French village in 1940 is a sIG.33/1 that has been converted on the chassis of a Pz.Kpfw.I *Ausf.*B. This vehicle, nicknamed the 'Bison', was one of the earliest self-propelled artillery pieces. It belonged to the 706 *Infanterie-Geschutz-Kompanie* 'Bison' and is painted in dark grey. Note the painted white 'K' identifying the machine as belonging to *Panzergruppe von Kleist*. The 'E' also painted in white indicates that it was the fifth gun within the battery. These guns were all identified as A through to F.

(**Above**) The crew of a sIG.33/1 'Bison' can be seen here loading ammunition. Ammunition for these vehicles was carried in the support vehicle as only three rounds could be carried on board the vehicle itself. Only thirty-eight of these vehicles were ever converted in early 1940 and employed with infantry gun companies.

During operations in France in 1940 a 'Bison' can be seen here on a cobbled road. Note the boxy 10mm-thick superstructure that was extremely high (3.5m), and the gun added almost 3 tons of weight to the chassis, making it very top-heavy with poor cross-country mobility. It had a five-man crew, two of whom rode in an accompanying Sd.Kf.10 half-track carrying ammunition.

A 'Bison' crewman wearing his black armoured uniform and beret standing in front of his machine. Crews sometimes referred to the vehicles as *Sturmpanzer* I, but generally in the field they were known as the 'Bison'.

(**Opposite, above**) During what appears to be an attack, infantry armed with their Karabiner 98k bolt-action rifles charge along a road in support of the sIG.33/1. The 'Bison' was used as a supporting infantry weapon and soldiers knew that using the new self-propelled artillery vehicles would ensure they could reach the front lines quickly and effectively without being left behind by the rapid advance of the Panzers. These self-propelled vehicles were normally attached to Panzer divisions.

(**Opposite, below**) During a halt in the advance a 'Bison' crewman can be seen next to his machine. Of interest, note the rear sections of the two side wall plates that were on hinges and could be opened to provide the crew with additional space on board and some protection while being resupplied with ammunition.

(**Above**) A 'Bison' advancing along a road with supporting vehicles following up in the rear. The driver's front plate had two visor ports, and a large hatch located to the front upper left served to provide a clear view for the gunner's ights.

(**Above**) An sIG.33/1 'Bison' enters a French village watched by infantry and a motorcyclist wearing his distinctive rubberized motorcycle coat. Note the letter 'A' painted on the side armour plate denoting the *Sturmpanzer* is the first vehicle in the battery.

(**Opposite, above**) A 'Bison' crossing a field during operations in France in 1940. The interior of these vehicles was cramped, and because of the large size of the ammunition only three rounds could be transported. This consequently limited the effectiveness of the gun, and while there were ammunition carriers supporting the batteries, the 'Bison' sometimes outran its supply lines. Frequently this resulted in crews storing additional rounds inside the vehicle.

(**Opposite, below**) The weight of the gun, the gun shield, ammunition and the crew often put great strain on the Pz.Kpfw.I *Ausf.*B suspension. Consequently a number of them broke down with suspension failures, as this photograph clearly shows.

(**Opposite, above**) Two sIG.33/1 'Bison' inside a French village in 1940. Note the vehicle behind. The crew has fabricated a tarp to help keep dust out of the gun port. The front vehicle has its muzzle plug in place. Most self-propelled guns used canvas muzzle covers rather than plugs. Part of the initial training of the crews, as standard procedure, was to visually inspect the bore to ensure there were no obstructions before firing.

(**Opposite, below**) A photograph showing two crewmen inside the cramped confines of their 'Bison' during a halt in their advance through France. The crew varied slightly from four to five men, but there were always two gun operators.

(**Above**) A 'Bison' is seen here at the side of the road getting much interest from passing infantry and support vehicles. It's probable that the vehicle has developed a mechanical problem as some reportedly overheated due to the speed of the operation. Because the sIG companies could not keep pace with the speed of the Panzers, it was advised that they should be attached to infantry divisions for future operational roles.

Infantry are seen here next to a 'Bison' that again appears to have developed some kind of mechanical fault, possibly a track issue. Most of the breakdowns were with transmission, clutch, brakes and the tracks.

A sIG.33/1 'Bison' advances along a French road, much to the interest of a group of soldiers and a motorcyclist standing at the side of the road watching the spectacle. Inside the vehicle the driver was positioned on the left side and was fully protected. The gunner was positioned to the left of the gun and the loader to the right of him. The gun-loader was often positioned behind them in order to reload at a moment's notice.

(**Above**) The 'Bison' were often given individual names by the crew and this 15cm sIG.33 is named Cambrai, probably following the successful battle that was fought there in France in 1940.

(**Opposite, above**) During operations in Greece and an sIG.33/1 'Bison' can be seen here negotiating uneven ground. The number '704' painted in white on the front of the vehicle denotes that the machine belongs to the *Infanterieschutz-Kompanie* 704 that was assigned to the 5th Panzer Division in April 1940. Note the Sd.Kz.10 behind the 'Bison' and the cyclist of a DKW NZ 350 motorcycle moving carefully alongside the sIG.

(**Opposite, below**) A 'Bison' of *Infanterieschutz-Kompanie* 704 advancing along a road after passing a line of headquarters vehicles. The crew has utilized a tarp to help keep dust and grime out of the gun port.

A 'Bison' crewman standing next to his machine. Note beneath the gun carriage the driver's front plate with its two visor ports. The upper front plates of the ports were slightly angled inwards in order to give the crew additional protection from small-arms fire and battlefield debris.

During operations on the Eastern Front in the summer of 1941, *Sturmpanzer* I passing an abandoned Red Army KV-2.

A 'Bison' has halted in a field in readiness for an attack against an enemy position. One of the crew members scans the terrain ahead trying to deduce and locate the whereabouts of his enemy. Note that the 15cm gun barrel is unplugged.

(**Above**) Belonging to the *Infanterieschutz-Kompanie* 706, this 'Bison', which was the fifth gun in the battery, can be seen advancing along a dusty road during operations on the Eastern Front in 1941. The 706 was attached to the 10th Panzer Division.

(**Opposite, above**) During operations on the Eastern Front in the summer of 1941 and a column of 'Bison' can be seen on the advance. Note how cramped the crew are on board the leading vehicle. Three wicker cases can be seen on the deck containing the ammunition.

(**Opposite, below**) During winter operations in Russia, a whitewashed 'Bison' can be seen advancing through deep snow.

On the Eastern Front and a whitewashed 'Bison' can be seen halted next to what appears to be a Pz.Kpfw.II. In late 1941 German supply lines were considerably overstretched, their vehicles were breaking down and casualty returns were mounting by the hour. The front soon stagnated in the snow.

Chapter Two

1942–43

By the end of 1941 the battle-weary divisions of the *Panzerwaffe* that had taken part in Operation BARBAROSSA were no longer fit to fight. Mobile operations had consequently ground to a halt. Fortunately for the exhausted armoured crews and supporting units, no mobile operations had been planned during the winter of 1941, let alone for 1942. In the freezing arctic temperatures the majority of the Panzer divisions were pulled out of their stagnant defensive positions and transferred to France to rest, reorganize and retrain. As for the self-propelled heavy infantry gun companies, their losses on the Eastern Front had been heavy. The 705th and 706th attached to the 7th and 10th Panzer divisions had been destroyed. The vehicles in the remaining companies had either developed mechanical problems, were knocked out of action or the remnants were too weak to operate effectively on the battlefield. Only the 701st was deemed battle-worthy and would eventually take part in the opening phase of the southern summer offensive, known as *Fall Blau* ('Case Blue'). As for the surviving crew members in the other companies, they would be absorbed into other armoured units or were relocated to the infantry school at Döberitz. There they trained and assisted with the formation of new units. However, training for the sIG.33 *auf* Pz.I would be short-lived. By the end of June 1943 only two vehicles remained operational in the 704th Company of the 5th Panzer Division.

While the sIG.33 *auf* Pz.I only saw limited success during its short operational time on the battlefield, in 1942 there was still a drastic requirement for further motorized artillery to be mounted on the chassis of other tanks. Improvements in design were quickly completed and various tank chassis were made available to be converted and sent to the front at a moment's notice. The Germans continued to utilize the powerful heavy field 15cm howitzer. One tank that was chosen was the Pz.Kpfw.II. The gun mount was initially bolted onto the chassis of an *Ausf.*B, but there was not enough space. Consequently the chassis was lengthened by 60cm, which required adding a sixth road wheel, and widened by 32cm to properly house the gun while still retaining a low silhouette; 15mm plates were also bolted to the front and sides of the open-topped fighting compartment, which was opened at the rear as well. Its sides were much lower than the front, but once again the crew was exposed to small-arms fire and shell fragments. Twelve of these new self-propelled artillery vehicles were built between late 1941 and January 1942. They were designated as the 15cm sIG 33 *auf fahrgestell Panzerkampfwagen* II (Sf), but occasionally referred to as the *Sturmpanzer* II 'Bison'. All these new vehicles were shipped to North Africa in 1942, where they operated in the 90th Light Afrika Division. They formed the *schwere Infanteriegeschütz-Kompanien (mot. S.)* ('Heavy Self-Propelled Infantry Gun Companies) 707 and 708, with the main task of close support for mobile artillery.

Once again, operations for these vehicles were limited and their impact on the battlefield did not have the desired effect against the enemy. By the end of 1942 eight of the vehicles were reported to have been knocked out of action, while British forces captured six of them that had been abandoned during the *Afrika-Korps* withdrawal.

It was noted that the *Sturmpanzer* II was mechanically unreliable on the battlefield and its weight of 16 tons meant that its engine was too weak. This consequently caused overheating. As a result further development of this self-propelled vehicle on the chassis of a Pz.Kpfw.II was abandoned. However, Field Marshal Erwin Rommel could see the advantage of motorized artillery in the desert campaign and demanded that a solution should be found. He was also aware of the great demand put on German engineers to repair self-propelled vehicles that had been damaged in action or had broken down. In order to get as many serviceable fighting vehicles as possible to the front lines, he concluded that working 15cm sIG heavy infantry guns from knocked-out self-propelled vehicles could be cannibalized from the battlefield and sent back into action with the converted gun on a new tank chassis. Consequently, the Pz.Kpfw.III *Ausf.*H chassis was chosen and modified. The vehicle had twice the heavy mount with greater length and width, and much better off-road performance. It was designated the 15cm sIG.33 L/11(Sf) *auf fahrgestell Panzerkampfwagen* III *Ausf.*H (Sf). The whole purpose of the vehicle was to support advancing infantry and tanks and to be able to destroy enemy defensive positions while under heavy fire. However, only one of them was ever modified.

Other self-propelled artillery vehicles were also used in North Africa, one of which was designated the LgsFH.13 (Sfl) *auf* Lorraine-Schlepper. The vehicle was nicknamed the *Geschützwagen*, which meant 'gun vehicle'. The 15cm sFH.13/1 howitzer was converted and bolted on top of a captured French army Lorraine 37L tracked Schlepper armoured transporter chassis. Production of these vehicles began in earnest in May 1942 and some ninety-four of them were eventually built. It was an unusual design, necessary because of the location of the engine, which resulted in its distinctive overhang shape. Rommel's *Afrika-Korps* was in desperate need of self-propelled artillery guns that could keep up with his fast-moving armour. The first of thirty Alkett-built 15cm sFH.13/1(Sf) *auf* GW Lorraine Schlepper (f) were shipped out to North Africa where they were distributed between three of the Panzer divisions. Twelve arrived for the 21st Panzer Division, while another twelve were dispatched to the 15th Panzer Division and the remaining six were sent to the 90th *Leicht* Division. Another twenty-three arrived two months later in July when they were immediately sent to the front lines. Each regiment comprised five batteries with six self-propelled artillery guns in each battery. They were distributed into the *Gepanzerte Artillerie-Regiment* 1 (Sfl) and the *Gepanzerte Artillerie-Regiment* 2 (Sfl). These regiments were very effective on the battlefield, and due to their numbers they achieved a number of successful engagements against the enemy. However, following months of sustaining heavy fighting against growing British firepower in the desert, losses among the *Geschützwagen* were high.

As a result, by late 1942 the *Gepanzerte Artillerie-Regiment* 1 (Sfl) was disbanded. By March 1943 the *Gepanzerte Artillerie-Regiment* 2 (Sfl) was reorganized and renamed *Artillerie-Regiment* 931 and then later, operating in the 21st Panzer Division, was designated *Panzer-Artillerie-Regiment* 155. However, within a year only twelve of the original thirty 15cm sFH.13/1 self-propelled vehicles were left operational.

The Lorraine-Schlepper had shown that mass production of a modified vehicle yielded quick results on the battlefield. It was these results that the *Panzerwaffe* urgently needed if it was to sustain its forces on the battlefield. As a result, 1942 led to a drastic need for further self-propelled artillery of other various tank chassis that could be rapidly converted. One of them was the 15cm sIG.33 (Sfl) *auf* Pz.Kpfw.38(t) *Grille* ('Bison') Sd.Kfz.138/1 self-propelled artillery gun that mounted the standard German 15cm heavy howitzer attached to the chassis of the obsolete Pz.Kpfw.38(t) *Ausf.*H. The first version of the *Grille* was converted on the *Ausf.*H Pz.Kpfw.38(t) chassis. The turret and the top plate of the superstructure were removed and the 15cm howitzer was mounted in their place. An enclosed gun shield was then built, with 25mm armour at the front and 15mm on the sides. The prototype *Grille* was completed by BMM in October 1942, but production of the vehicle did not commence until February 1943. Some ninety *Ausf.*H chassis were converted. At the same time modifications were being made for the *Ausf.*M chassis, specifically for use with the 15cm gun. However, the final version was known as the Marder III and this became known as a tank-hunter.

The *Ausf.*H was issued to heavy infantry gun units of *Panzergrenadier* and Panzer divisions, with every detachment having six vehicles in each platoon. They were sent to the Eastern Front and Italy, and some operated in the defence of Normandy in 1944. Once again the self-propelled artillery platoons operated well, but as always they were hindered by the limited numbers produced.

In 1943, which was regarded as the watershed for the production of self-propelled artillery, Hitler was eager to change the course of how operations were conducted on the battlefield by increasing the production of motorized artillery. The deadly

15cm howitzer had demonstrated over the last couple of years how versatile it was to convert. As a result, in early 1943 a large self-propelled vehicle was converted and was nicknamed the *Hummel*, but initially called the 'Bumblebee'. It was designated the *Panzerfeldhaubitze* 18M *auf Geschützwagen* III/IV (Sf) *Hummel*, Sd.Kfz.165. Although the vehicle was designed in late 1942, it was not until early the following year that minor alterations to the design were made such as mounting the more powerful 15cm sFH.18 L/30 howitzer on the specially-converted chassis of a Pz.Kpfw.III/IV. In order to allow for the open-topped lightly-armoured fighting compartment to be bolted onto the tank and give room for the crew to fire the gun, the engine was moved to the centre of the vehicle. Various modifications to the *Hummel* were made during the war by slightly altering the driver's compartment and front superstructure. Generally the vehicle remained the same throughout its operational time on the battlefield. One drawback of the design was that it could only carry limited amounts of ammunition due to the restricted amount of space in the fighting compartment. In order to overcome this problem, a *Munitionsträger Hummel* ('munitions carrier *Hummel*') was produced. The carrier was basically a standard production *Hummel* without the mounted 15cm gun. It contained racks of ammunition, but what made this vehicle unique was that it could be easily converted into a fully-fledged fighting vehicle while operating on the battlefield.

By the early summer of 1943 the *Hummel* made its appearance on the Eastern Front. Every third battery of each armoured artillery regiment was supplied with six *Hummels*. At the end of June eighty-five of these new vehicles were sent to the front. Although two *Hummel* ammunition carriers were planned for each battery, many of them, especially during the initial stages, operated with only one, which consequently limited their fighting capacity.

The *Hummel*'s emergence in the order of battle against Russia had come at the right time. By this point in the war the *Panzerwaffe* were hard-pressed against their irrepressible foe. The German soldier had expended considerable combat efforts while lacking sufficient reconnaissance and the necessary support of tanks and heavy weapons to ensure any type of success. The Red Army had constantly outgunned them, and Luftwaffe air support was almost non-existent in a number of areas of the front. The short summer nights had also caused considerable problems for the men, for they only had a few hours of darkness in which to conceal their night marches and the construction of field fortifications. Ultimately, the German soldier in the summer of 1943 was ill-prepared to launch a massive offensive in the East, even with considerable support from Panzers and new self-propelled artillery. Yet, despite the gloomy outlook, Hitler was to gamble his armour in Russia in a large-scale offensive known as the Battle of Kursk. The offensive was the *Hummel*'s debut and around a hundred of them served in armoured artillery battalions or *Panzerartillerie-Abteilungen* of the Panzer divisions.

Although the Battle of Kursk was a failure for the Germans, the *Hummel* proved its worth in action in spite of ammunition supply problems, but it was not just the *Hummel*'s debut at Kursk that was an accomplishment in new self-propelled artillery design and power. The introduction of the vehicle known as the *Sturmpanzer* and designated the *Sturmpanzer* 43 or Sd.Kfz.166 was a machine designed purely to offer direct infantry fire support, especially during urbanized fighting. The vehicle was a converted Pz.Kpfw.IV utilizing the tank's upper hull and turret space by replacing it by a new casemate-style armoured superstructure that housed a powerful 15cm (5.9in) *Sturmhaubitze* (StuH) 43 L/12 gun. It fired the same shells as the 15cm sIG.33 heavy infantry gun. The vehicle was commonly known by the nickname of *Brummbär*. Production of the first series of vehicles began in earnest in April 1943. Of the sixty produced, fifty-two were built using the new Pz.Kpfw.IV *Ausf.*G chassis, while the remaining eight were rebuilt from *Ausf.*E and F chassis. The vehicles were then sent to Amiens for new crews to train for battle. The unit was organized into *Sturmpanzer-Abteilung* 216, where it was prepared into three line companies, each with fourteen vehicles, and a battalion headquarters with three vehicles. Following a few weeks of training, the unit was deemed battle-ready and sent by train to central Russia in order to prepare for the Battle of Kursk. For the offensive, '216' was provisionally assigned as the third battalion of *Schwere Panzerjäger Regiment* 656 ('Heavy Anti-Tank Regiment 656') under the command of the 9th Army of Army Group Centre. Operations by the *Brummbär* in the Orel-Bryansk area were successful, but limited due to considerable Russian defensive lines. By the end of August 1943 the unit was sent to Dnepropetrovsk-Zaporozhye where it fought a number of defensive battles. Apart from limited success on the battlefield, it soon became obvious that the vehicles, with an ammunition load of thirty-eight shells, a five-man crew and a fighting weight of 28.2 tons, were heavily overloaded. Yet in spite of this the vehicles were refitted until they were finally withdrawn from the Dnepropetrovsk-Zaporozhye area in October.

With various self-propelled artillery now fighting extensively along the Eastern Front, the Germans hoped that vehicles like the *Brummbär*, *Hummel* and *Grille* with their heavy motorized infantry guns would contribute decisively against the Red Army. However, there was one vehicle introduced in 1943 that was the most famous and durable of them all in combat. It was the Sd.Kfz.124 *Wespe* ('Wasp') and designated the *Leichte Feldhaubitze* 18/2 *auf fahrgestell Panzerkampfwagen* II (Sf) ('Light field howitzer 18 on Panzer II chassis self-propelled'). Although this vehicle was not as mass-produced as the *Hummel*, it was the most versatile and successful. Designs first began following the Battle of France where commanders in the field had deemed that the Pz.Kpfw.II was under-gunned and under-armoured. However, the chassis was deemed perfect for providing mobility to an artillery gun. It was therefore decided that the famous standard German infantry 10.5cm leFH.18 howitzer would be bolted to the chassis of a Pz.Kpfw.II *Ausf.*F variant. Modifications were made to the tank's engine and it was moved forward, while the chassis was slightly lengthened to house the rear-mounted 10.5cm gun. The superstructure was lightly-armoured and left open at the top and rear. The armoured plate was only 10mm thick, but deemed sufficient to block enemy small-arms fire. Production of the vehicle began in February 1943 and continued until June 1944. Some 676 had been produced during that time, with an additional 159 gunless *Wespes* manufactured to serve as mobile artillery ammunition carriers.

The vehicles were allocated to the armoured artillery battalions or *Panzerartillerie Abteilungen* of the Panzer divisions and fought alongside the heavier *Hummel*. The first of these *Wespe* battalions made their debut on the Eastern Front in March 1943. Alongside the *Hummel* the *Wespe* saw extensive action at Kursk in July. During combat the *Wespe* proved reliable and highly manoeuvrable, but losses to crews were high due to inadequate protection; however, in spite of the casualties the vehicle enjoyed considerable success. However, by late 1943 self-propelled artillery units on the Eastern Front were overstretched and required to support the dwindling Panzers. The coming months would prove decisive for German armour.

A 15cm sIG.33 *auf Fahrgestell* Pz.Kpw.II(Sf), incorrectly identified as a 'Bison' II, probably seen before deployment to North Africa. These vehicles, with the powerful 15cm sIG.33 L/12 heavy gun mounted on the chassis of a Pz.Kpfw.II, were used as direct-fire artillery in support of assaulting infantry. Twelve were built in late 1941 and January 1942.

Operating in North Africa and two 15cm sIG.33 *auf Fahrgestell* Pz.Kpw.II(Sf) can be seen here moving through a town. These vehicles served with the 707 and 708 *Schwere Infanteriegeschutze Kompanien*.

Out in the North African desert and the crew of this 15cm sIG.33 *auf Fahrgestell* Pz.Kpw.II(Sf) can be seen here with their vehicle. The gun had a 75° elevation. Only ten rounds were carried on board and it had a crew of four. However, because of its low profile, the crew found that they had insufficient protection.

A battery of 15cm sIG.33 *auf Fahrgestell* Pz.Kpw.II(Sf) halted out in the field during operations in North Africa. The crew found that the vehicle's cross-country mobility was not good, mainly due to the fact that the engine was underpowered.

A 15cm sFH.13/1(Sf) *auf Geschützwagen Lorraine Schlepper* (f) self-propelled howitzer (Sd.Kfz.135/1) can be seen here in North Africa. These infantry-supporting vehicles, built on captured French Lorraine tractor chassis, were first used in North Africa, mainly by the 15th and 21st Panzer divisions. Note the application of camouflage paint sprayed over the body and 15cm gun. It appears to be sand colour painted over dark grey.

A 15cm sFH.13/1(Sf) *auf Geschützwagen Lorraine Schlepper* (f) is halted in the field with its 15cm howitzer elevated in preparation for a fire mission. The howitzer had a very limited traverse of 5° left and right with a 40° elevation.

An abandoned 15cm sFH.13/1(Sf) *auf Geschützwagen Lorraine Schlepper* (f) in Libya in 1943. When these vehicles first arrived in North Africa, thirty were dispatched to the *Gepanzerte Artillerie-Regiment* 1 (Sfl) and another thirty to the *Gepanzerte Artillerie-Regiment* 2 (Sfl). Each regiment comprised five batteries with six self-propelled guns in each. However, by the end of 1942 *Gepanzerte Artillerie-Regiment* 1 (Sfl) was disbanded and sent to infantry divisions stationed in the West. The *Gepanzerte Artillerie-Regiment* 2 (Sfl) was then reorganized in early 1943 and renamed *Artillerie-Regiment* 931 and later *Panzer-Artillerie-Regiment* 155, all of which operated in the 21st Panzer Division.

A 15cm sFH.13/1(Sf) *auf Geschützwagen Lorraine Schlepper* (f) during a training exercise, probably in France in 1943. This vehicle had initially been part of the disbanded *Gepanzerte Artillerie-Regiment* 1 (Sfl) in North Africa.

A photograph taken in 1943 showing a 15cm sIG.33(Sf) *auf* Pz.Kpfw.38(t) *Grille* ('Cricket') *Ausf.*H, (Sd.Kfz.138/1). These vehicles were built on the chassis of a Pz.Kpfw.38(t) and mounted a 15cm sIG.33/1 L12 infantry gun. They were produced in limited numbers and with service on all fronts, assigned to *Panzergrenadier* regiments.

The first photograph is part of a battery of 15cm sFH.13/1(Sf) *auf Geschützwagen Lorraine Schlepper* (f) being serviced by the crew in France. Note the driver's compartment is open with its split shutters opening upward and downward. Also visible is the MG 34 machine gun with an anti-aircraft sight mounted on the right front of the superstructure of the first vehicle. The second image shows the crew posing in front of the *Lorraine Schlepper* (f).

A 15cm sIG.33(Sf) *auf* Pz.Kpfw. 38(t) *Grille Ausf.*H can be seen here moving along a road at speed during operations on the Eastern Front. The superstructure of this vehicle was built around the sIG.33 howitzer, which was open-topped. Its design made the crew vulnerable to enemy fire. The majority of the ammunition was stored on the superstructure walls due to restricted space, while other rounds were stored in the hull.

Here a 15cm sIG.33(Sf) *auf* Pz.Kpfw.38(t) *Grille Ausf.*H is halted on a road in front of an Sd.Kfz.10 during operations in Italy. The vehicle had a crew of five and was provided with an MG 34 carried in the gun compartment. They were used in support of *Panzergrenadiers* along the front.

A battery of 15cm sIG.33(Sf) *auf* Pz.Kpfw.38(t) *Grille Ausf.*H on the Eastern Front. Each detachment in the *Schwere Infanteriegeschütz* companies within the *Panzergrenadier* regiments had six of these vehicles.

A crew member standing in front of his *Grille Ausf.*H. Around ninety-one of these *Ausf.*H variants were produced between February and April 1943. Although the vehicles had disadvantages, the *Wehrmacht* was able to field fast-moving 15cm field howitzers along the front. As with all self-propelled artillery, the vehicles had the tactical ability to fire off a round and then quickly relocate to another position without encountering any return fire.

A battery of whitewashed *Grilles* with their 15cm guns elevated in preparation for a fire mission on the Eastern Front in 1943. In the winter the open-air compartment exposed the crews to the extreme Russian weather conditions.

Stationary here on the Eastern Front is the 15cm *Schwere Panzerhaubitze auf Geschützwagen* III/IV(Sf) or Sd.Kfz.165, commonly known as the *Hummel* ('Bumblebee'). This revolutionary self-propelled vehicle was based on the chassis of the Pz.Kpfw.III/IV and armed with the powerful 15cm howitzer. The *Hummel* was designed in 1942 following the drastic need for more mobile artillery support for the *Panzerwaffe* on the Eastern Front.

Shirtless *Hummel* crewmen can be seen here standing on their stationary vehicle during a pause in action. When this self-propelled vehicle was built it was first believed that it could drastically change the way in which motorized artillery operated on the battlefield and move faster than the tanks. However, it achieved neither of these things. Its top speed was roughly the same as the Pz.Kpfw.IV and it had a 30° traverse. Although up to 705 *Hummels* were reportedly built during the war, it was regarded as an interim vehicle until something better was developed.

(**Above**) A *Hummel* operating in Italy can be seen here advancing through a town. The first *Hummels* entered service in March 1943 and were immediately sent to the Eastern Front to give much-needed artillery support to the Panzer divisions. Note one of the crewmen perched on the 15cm sFH.18 L/30 heavy field howitzer.

(**Opposite, above**) The crew of a stationary *Hummel* poses for the camera. Note the canvas muzzle cover and the large 'A'-frame travel-lock bracket that was mounted on the front hull glacis armoured plate. This was locked in place when the vehicle's gun was not in use. The bracket also stabilized the gun while travelling across rough ground.

(**Opposite, below**) Two *Hummels* can be seen here operating on the Eastern Front. The crew has applied foliage to the vehicle in order to break up its distinctive shape and help protect it from both aerial and ground reconnaissance.

A *Hummel* advancing along a dirt track during operations in Russia. The vehicle was operated by a crew of six comprising the commander, driver and four gunners. They were protected by an enclosed high-silhouette armoured fighting compartment. Although it had an open-topped fighting compartment, in order to protect the crew from the often harsh weather conditions they were issued with a tarpaulin cover. Note the letter 'E' painted in yellow on the side of the fighting compartment indicating that it's the fifth gun in the battery.

A Waffen-SS *Hummel* battery on the front line during operations on the Eastern Front. Both the *Wehrmacht* and Waffen-SS Panzer divisions had their own heavy self-propelled artillery batteries that were part of their artillery regiment battalions. The *Hummel* made its debut at Kursk in July 1943, and from then until the end of the war they were operated by the Panzer artillery regiments. *(NARA)*

Two photographs showing gunners preparing their *Hummel* for a fire mission. The *Hummel*'s 15cm high-explosive shells came in two parts. The explosive shell was loaded first, followed by the variable-charge canister. As a result of this firing procedure the *Hummel* could only carry eighteen rounds of shells. Expenditure of ammunition could often be quick if the battle was ongoing and for this reason the *Hummel* included an ammunition-carrying *Munitionsträger*. On the battlefield they were formed into separate heavy self-propelled artillery batteries, each with six *Hummels* and one *Munitionsträger* version.

(**Above**) A crew member relaxing on board a *Hummel* on a dirt road. With the Panzer divisions already stretched along a huge front, the *Hummel* did what it could to support the dwindling lines. As a consequence the vehicle suffered such a high loss rate that many divisions could not replace them.

(**Opposite, above**) A *Hummel* advancing towards the front across typical Russian terrain. This vehicle gave the Panzer divisions the heavy punch they needed when mounting counter-attacks. However, there were never enough *Hummels* produced to repel the enemy and support the overstretched *Panzerwaffe*.

(**Opposite, below**) A Waffen-SS *Hummel* can be seen here advancing along a road. Note the national flag erected inside the fighting compartment. This was done for recognition purposes. The vehicle is also carrying camouflage netting as well, which can be seen draped over the gun barrel.

(**Above**) A *Hummel* can be seen here advancing through a devastated Russian town. By this period of the war much of the burden had fallen on the assault artillery and tank-destroyer battalions to try to stem the Red Army onslaught.

(**Opposite, above**) A *Hummel* shown during winter operations. By late 1943 self-propelled artillery was continually hard-pressed on the battlefield and constantly called on for offensive and defensive fire support, where it was gradually compelled to increasingly operate in an anti-tank role, a purpose for which these vehicles were not intended.

(**Opposite, below**) Seen here stationary in a field is a *Hummel* flanked by a *Sturmgeschütz* III complete with side-skirts. Within months of entering service the *Hummel* played a prominent role in the desperate attempt to halt the Soviet onslaught. Even though these powerful artillery vehicles were vastly outnumbered, they were ultimately a credit to the Panzer divisions they served.

Two *Hummel* crewmen posing for the camera in front of their vehicle. Note camouflage netting draped over the 15cm gun barrel.

Two photographs showing *Hummels* being loaded onto flatbed railway cars destined for the front line. Moving vehicles by rail became a common requirement by the *Panzerwaffe* in late 1943. It enabled the Panzer divisions to move from one front to another quickly and effectively without inflicting wear and tear on the vehicles.

A battery of camouflaged *Hummels* preparing for a fire mission on the Eastern Front. Often these vehicles remained away from the front lines which enabled them to fire their guns some 10 miles into enemy positions, allowing Panzer and other armoured vehicles to then move forward into action.

Hummel crew members can be seen here posing for the camera during a pause in operations in southern Russia.

A battery of whitewashed *Hummels* with their 15cm guns elevated in preparation for a fire mission during winter operations on the Eastern Front.

A *Hummel* can be seen here advancing through a town. Note four of the crew members inside the open-topped fighting compartment. Of further interest is the fuel drum that can be seen wedged on the front of the vehicle between a spare wheel and what appears to be the fighting compartment tarpaulin. The vast distances over which these vehicles were compelled to travel meant that quite often tracked vehicles outstripped their fuel supplies, prompting the crews to carry reserves.

(**Opposite, above**) A battery of *Hummels* somewhere on the Eastern Front with their 15cm gun barrels elevated during a fire mission against an enemy target.

(**Opposite, below**) A *Hummel* out in the field flanked by a stationary Sd.Kfz.251 personnel carrier. The vehicle is fully laden with supplies including a wooden locker box attached to the front of the vehicle. Foliage has also been applied to the *Hummel*. Note the 'A'-frame travel-lock bracket mounted on the front hull glacis armoured plate, which has been unlocked by the crew for a fire mission so they can traverse the gun barrel.

(**Above**) In thick snow a member of a 15cm *Hummel* gun crew uses a field telephone to call the fire control centre. The *Hummel*, which has received a nice full coat of winter whitewash paint, is marked with the letter 'G', denoting the gun's place within the battery.

A *Hummel* utilizing a windmill as concealment on open ground during winter operations. The vehicle appears to be painted in a dark grey or green. Note the very small *Balkenkreuz* ('bar cross') painted on the side of the vehicle in order to make it less noticeable for the enemy to use as an aiming-point.

A stationary whitewashed *Hummel* can be seen halted in a field with two of its crew members standing next to it.

During the Kursk offensive in July 1943, this photograph shows the *Sturmpanzer*, also known as the *Sturmpanzer* 43 or Sd.Kfz.166, which was an infantry support gun bolted onto the chassis of a Pz.Kpw.IV. German soldiers nicknamed it the *Stupa*. For the Kursk attack these vehicles were initially assigned to the third battalion of *Schwere Panzerjäger Regiment* 656 under the command of the 9th Army of Army Group Centre.

A *Sturmpanzer* 43 on the advance during operations in Russia in the summer of 1943. The vehicle, using a Pz.Kpfw.IV chassis, had the upper hull and turret replaced with a new casemate-style armoured superstructure housing a 15cm *Sturmhaubitze* (StuH) 43 L/12 developed by Škoda. It fired the same shells as the 15cm sIG.33 heavy infantry gun.

(**Opposite, above**) What appears to be a photograph taken during the Battle of Kursk in July 1943 and a *Sturmpanzer 43* can be seen with a Tiger I. For the attack these powerful vehicles were organized into three line companies, each with fourteen vehicles, and a battalion headquarters with three vehicles. It arrived in Central Russia on 10 June 1943.

(**Opposite, below**) An Sd.Kfz.124 *Wespe* ('Wasp'), also known as the *Leichte Feldhaubitze* 18/2 *auf Fahrgestell Panzerkampfwagen* II (Sf) ('Light field howitzer 18 on Panzer II chassis (self-propelled'). This photograph was taken of a *Wespe* on the battlefield in the summer of 1943. This popular vehicle was armed with a 10.5cm leFH.18/2 L/28 gun and protected by a lightly-armoured superstructure mounted on the chassis of a Pz.Kpfw.II. This vehicle served in armoured artillery battalions, but they were lightly-armoured and as a result many of them were lost in battle.

(**Above**) A *Sturmpanzer* which appears to have been knocked out of action during operations in Italy. This vehicle probably belongs to *Sturmpanzer-Abteilung* 216 (Stu.Pz.Abt.216) which was transferred in early February. Note the thick coating of Zimmerit anti-magnetic mine paste.

(**Above**) A well-concealed *Wespe* in a field. The commander can be seen scouring the terrain ahead through a pair of Zeiss binoculars.

(**Opposite, below**) A Waffen-SS *Wespe* operating during the Battle of Kursk. The 10.5cm leFH.18/2 L/28 gun had a 17° left and right traverse and a 42° elevation. While the crew was often armed with their Karabiner 98k bolt-action rifles, they were provided with an MG 34 machine gun for local defence. This gun was sometimes mounted atop the fighting compartment on the right side. (*NARA*)

(**Above**) A crewman converses with an infantryman from his *Wespe* open-topped fighting compartment during operations on the Eastern Front. These vehicles were built on a Pz.Kpfw.II *Ausf.*F variant chassis modified by relocating the engine in a central position to allow space for the gun compartment.

A column of *Wespe* belonging to the *Grossdeutschland* Division during operations at Kursk in July 1943. This particular photograph was taken in Ponyri.

A battery of Waffen-SS *Wespe* belonging to the *Leibstandarte* Division can be seen here in a field with their gun barrels elevated in preparation for a fire mission on the Eastern Front. Note in the distance a *Hummel* supporting the action. It was in 1943 that one of the artillery batteries was upgraded with *Wespes* and *Hummels*. The *Leibstandarte* Division was the first Waffen-SS unit to receive the *Wespe*. (NARA)

A battery of *Wespes* on the Eastern Front preparing for a fire mission along a broad front.

Two photographs showing a *Wespe* of SS Panzer-Artillery Regiment 10 from the 10th SS Panzer Division *Frundsberg* while they were stationed in France in late 1943. These vehicles were issued to artillery regiments of the Panzer and *Panzergrenadier* divisions.

A *Wespe* belonging to an artillery regiment with the 2nd Panzer Division on the Eastern Front. The *Wespe* brought greater mobility to the artillery formations of the Panzer divisions and were often seen fighting along with heavier *Hummel* self-propelled artillery.

A column of *Wespes* seen advancing through a town. The vehicle's superstructure, like so many of those among the self-propelled armour, was lightly-armoured with 10mm armour-plating. This was deemed sufficient to prevent small-arms fire penetrating the fighting compartment and killing or injuring the gunners.

Two photographs taken in sequence showing an artillery battalion's workshop company working in the field during operations in Italy. A *Wespe* crew is replacing a worn-out 10.5cm howitzer and an Sd.Kfz.9/1 half-track can be seen assisting.

Seen here out in the snow is a Waffen-SS *Wespe* that has received a full whitewash coating. Additional ammunition for these vehicles was carried in munitions *Sf auf Fgst* Pz.Kpfw.II or *Munitionsschlepper Wespe* fully-tracked carriers. Two of these carriers were used per battery. Only 159 of them were ever built, and a variety of vehicles sometimes carried them including the Sd.Kfz.6 or cargo trucks. *(NARA)*

A whitewashed *Wespe* operating in the snow. A typical *Wespe* battery comprised six guns. Slit trenches for the crews were often dug either next to or behind the gun, as depicted in this photograph.

A photograph taken at the moment that a *Wespe* fired its shell during an action in a field on the Eastern Front. The gun is in full recoil following the fire action.

A *Wespe* battery shown in a close firing position. Often these vehicles were positioned in tight formation, allowing the guns to deliver a close concentration of fire on a small target without having to adjust the angle of each gun.

An unidentified Waffen-SS *Wespe* battery during winter operations. The vehicles are in formation and in preparation for a fire mission against a Russian target. *(NARA)*

A *Wespe* crew at a training ground pose for the camera with their machine at a workshop prior to deployment to the Eastern Front.

Four photographs taken in sequence showing the *Wurfrahmen* 40 ('launch frame 40') being attached to an Sd.Kz.251 half-track. Although not technically self-propelled artillery, it is still worth noting. The weapon was rocket artillery that was highly mobile and more versatile in battle than the towed *Nebelwerfer* ('smoke mortar'). In these photographs the *Nebelwerfer* crew is carrying the weapon system complete in its framework with adjustable base plates that were fitted over and alongside the vehicle. However, due to its weight and reloading time, the use of this weapon was regarded as unfeasible, but it was still used in a support mobile artillery role for Panzer formations, especially during urban operations. *(BA/Bender)*

Chapter Three

The End: 1944–45

By 1944 the *Panzerwaffe* was duty-bound to improvise with what they had at their disposal and try to maintain themselves in the field, and in doing so they hoped to wear down the enemy's offensive capability. Yet despite the dire situation in which they found themselves, German tanks including self-propelled anti-tank, anti-aircraft and motorized artillery units were still infused with confidence and the ability to hold their ground. Bleak as the circumstances were, armoured units were compelled to try to fill the gaps left by the infantry and hold the front to the grim death. Throughout early 1944 self-propelled artillery units fought well and were regarded as a significant contribution to the Panzer force. Although handicapped from the outset by their lack of reserves, they continued to try to hold their ground. Again and again various armoured units fought to the death.

By April, mud finally brought an end to the almost continuous fighting in the south and there was a respite for the *Panzerwaffe* in some areas of the front. Once more, despite the setbacks, there was a genuine feeling of motivation within the ranks of the *Panzerwaffe*. There was a renewed determination to detain the Red Army from reaching the Homeland. In addition, confidence was further bolstered by the efforts of the armaments industry as they began producing many new vehicles for the Eastern Front. In fact, during 1944 the *Panzerwaffe* was better supplied with equipment than during any other time on the Eastern Front, thanks to the armaments industry. In total some 20,000 fighting vehicles including 8,328 medium and heavy tanks, 5,751 assault guns, 3,617 tank destroyers and 1,246 self-propelled artillery vehicles of various types reached the Eastern Front. Included in these new arrivals were the second generation of tank-destroyers: the *Jagdpanzer* IV, followed by the *Hetzer* and then the *Jagdpanther* and *Jagdtiger*. By this late period of the war tank-destroyers, assault guns and self-propelled artillery, PaK and flak guns would soon outnumber the tanks, which was confirmation of the *Panzerwaffe*'s determination to perform a defensive role against overwhelming opposition. All these vehicles would have to be irrevocably stretched along a very thin Eastern Front, with many of them rarely reaching the proper operational level. Panzer divisions too were often broken up and split among hastily-constructed battle groups or *Kampfgruppen* drawn from a motley collection of armoured formations, but still these battle groups were put into the line while operating well below strength. The demands put upon the *Panzerwaffe* during the spring and summer of 1944 were immeasurable, and this constant employment, coupled with the nightmare of not having enough supplies, would have worried commanders in the field. The Red Army, encouraged by the Germans' dire situation, now mounted bolder operations aimed directly at the German front. Although German armour appeared stronger than ever, Soviet armaments production saw 29,000 tanks and assault guns being produced for the front lines in 1944, which put increasing strain on motorized artillery. Vehicles like the *Hummel* and *Wespe*, which were still deployed within the artillery regiments and particularly appreciated for their mobility and firepower capabilities, were now mounting counter-attacks with tank-destroyer units and new formidable machines like the Tiger E and the King Tiger B. However, production of the new second generation of tanks did nothing to alleviate the overall problems along the entire battered and worn Eastern Front. With too few of them being delivered, losses mounted including those of the *Hummel* and *Wespe*, which were often exposed out on the battlefield.

Between June and September 1944 the Germans had sustained around 1 million casualties. To make good their losses, many of the exhausted undermanned divisions were conscripted from among old men and low-grade troops. Also many of the replacement self-propelled artillery crews who did not have sufficient time to be properly trained found themselves being killed in action. Lack of fuel and insufficient spare parts coupled with the lack of trained crews all played a major part in reducing the effectiveness of the motorized artillery in the final year of the war.

As a consequence, the Red Army was able to spearhead its forces westward and use extremely rapid mobile units. By using heavy motorization it relieved the physical responsibility of the infantry, something the Germans had tried but were over-stretched. In many areas the Russians met with almost no resistance. During their almost unhindered drive they were able to cross Poland, advance towards Warsaw and cut off the main Siedlce railway lines. The capture of these lines severely delayed the tank, tank-destroyer and motorized artillery units from receiving reinforcements and ammunition. Consequently much of the ammunition had to be brought by road, risking the support columns being attacked by Red Army fighter-bombers that dominated the skies.

While fighting raged on the Eastern Front, in other theatres of operation mobile artillery batteries continued supporting both infantry and armoured attacks. In Italy the *Brummbär* played a major role in the planned counter-attack against the Allied beachhead at Anzio in early 1944. *Sturmpanzer-Abteilung* 216 had twenty-eight vehicles that participated in the attack. Although its operation failed, the battalion remained in Italy and continued to be heavily embroiled in a number of major battles.

In France the *Brummbär* saw fighting in Normandy, with seventeen *Sturmpanzers* belonging to *Sturmpanzer-Abteilung* 217 seeing action around the city of Caen.

However, a number of the vehicles had broken down during its march to the front. Luckily for the battalion, it was not trapped in the Falaise pocket and withdrew to the north-east of France. Later in the war on the Western Front the *Sturmpanzer* was sent to the Ardennes to participate in the offensive, but the roads and terrain were unsuited to the vehicle and its advance was limited. *Sturmpanzer-Abteilung* 217 then retreated and was finally captured in the Ruhr pocket in April 1945.

During the German defence of Poland in the summer of 1944 *Sturmpanzer-Kompanie zbV* 218, comprising a number of *Sturmpanzers*, was sent to Warsaw where it was attached to *Panzer Abteilung (Fkl)* 302. The company remained on the Eastern Front after the Warsaw Uprising was suppressed, but was totally destroyed during defensive operations in East Prussia during the last weeks of the war.

In Hungary around ten *Brummbär* fought during the defence of Hungary in late 1944. The vehicle formed *Sturmpanzer-Abteilung* 219 and was engaged in some heavy combat in and around Budapest. However, the remaining vehicles were forced to withdraw before overwhelming Russian superiority.

On all three German fronts self-propelled artillery batteries tried to contain the enemy. The *Hummel* and *Wespe* were seen extensively during the last year of the war engaged in heavy fighting. Even the *Lorraine Schlepper (f)* saw heavy action. During D-Day, three battalions of the *Panzer-Artillerie-Regiment* 155 of the 21st Panzer Division were equipped with a total of twenty-four 10.5cm leFH.18/40 *auf Geschütz-wagen Lorraine Schlepper (f)* (4th, 5th, 7th and 8th batteries), and twelve 15cm sFH.13 Geschützwagen Lorraine Schlepper(f) (6th and 9th batteries) self-propelled artillery gun conversions. Although the vehicles were initially successful and boasted no losses, by August 1944 all of them were eventually knocked out of action.

Despite fervent efforts to amplify the combat strength of the *Panzerwaffe* by increasing self-propelled artillery and *Panzerjäger* units, the crews were too exhausted to reverse the situation decisively. As a result, the fronts caved in and retreated back to the German Homeland. Along whole areas of the front the motorized artillery batteries had been reduced to skeletal formations on a stricken field. They were now not only vastly outnumbered but seriously lacked fuel supplies, lubricants and ammunition. When parts of the front were abandoned, armoured formations were often forced to destroy their equipment so that nothing was left for use by the conquering enemy. The Germans no longer had the manpower, war plant or transportation to accomplish a proper build-up of forces. Commanders could do little to compensate for the deficiencies, and in many sectors of the front they did not have any coherent planning in the event that the defence failed. During the last days of the war, most of the remaining motorized artillery comprised no more than *ad hoc* units simply thrown together in a fanatical defence. Although it saw extensive action, its success was limited and localized and did nothing to avert the enemy operations.

(**Above**) The crew of a *Hummel* can be seen here with their whitewashed vehicle on a special flatbed train destined for the front. The *Panzerwaffe* relied heavily on rail for transportation. Maintaining the momentum of an advance was vital to success and, without often sending whole units or even divisions to the front quickly, the whole advance might stall. In fact, not only did it save time over the huge distances that had to be covered, but it also allowed Panzer divisions to move from one part of the front to another quickly and effectively, and the main factor attributed to the success of the Panzer divisions' speed and mobility was rail transport.

(**Opposite, below**) Here on the Eastern Front is a partly whitewashed *Hummel* during a fire mission. Note the gun crew carrying the propellant canisters in preparation for firing the 15cm gun. *(BA/Bender)*

(**Opposite, below**) A well-concealed *Wespe* during defensive operations near Nettuno in Italy in March 1944. *(BA/Bender)*

(**Opposite, above**) A whitewashed *Hummel* on the Eastern Front in 1944. The 15cm gun has been elevated for a fire mission. Although these self-propelled vehicles were used successfully in Russia, by mid-1944 they were replaced by tank-destroyers.

(**Opposite, below**) A whitewashed Waffen-SS *Wespe* during winter operations on the Eastern Front. The *Wespe* was widely used in both the *Wehrmacht* and Waffen-SS on all fronts between 1943 and 1945. The main Panzer divisions in which they operated were the 1st, 2nd, 3rd, 4th, 5th, 6th, 7th, 8th, 9th, 11th, 12th, 13th, 14th, 16th, 17th, 19th, 20th, 23rd, 24th, 25th, 26th, 116th, *Feldherrnhalle*, *Tatra*, *Grossdeutschland*, 1st SS *Leibstandarte SS LAH*, 2nd SS *Das Reich*, 3rd SS *Totenkopf*, 5th SS *Wiking*, 9th SS *Hohenstaufen*, 10th SS *Frundsberg* and the 12th SS *Hitlerjugend*. There were also other divisions, such as the 7th *Freiwilligen Gebirgsjäger Division Prinz Eugen*, *Panzergrenadier Division Brandenburg*, *Fallschirmjäger-Panzer Division Hermann Göring* and the *Führer* Grenadier Division and Panzer Brigade West. (*NARA*)

(**Above**) An example of close coordination firing, and these whitewashed *Wespes* can be seen in action with their 10.5cm barrels elevated. Although difficult to see in the photograph, the rear drop tailgates are down in order to give the gunners more room while undertaking their fire mission and make it easier for the gun's 10.5cm projectiles to be loaded on board.

(**Opposite, above**) A captured *Hummel* that has fallen into Russian hands in 1944. The vehicle would have been painted in summer colours of dark yellow with a camouflage scheme of red-brown and olive green with wavy lines.

(**Opposite, below**) A captured *Wespe* somewhere on the Eastern Front. Although these self-propelled guns were scoring sizable successes in Russia, by mid-1944 the Allied bombing campaign was causing severe problems and shortages of fuel and spare parts were beginning to cripple the *Panzerwaffe*. By the end of the war only a handful of *Wespe* machines were captured intact.

(**Above**) Some crew members posing for the camera with their *Sturm-Infanteriegeschütz* 33B ('Assault Infantry Gun 33B'). The superstructure was built on the chassis of the *Sturmgeschütz* III. It mounted the improved sIG.33/1 infantry gun, offset to the right side. The gun could only traverse 3° to left and right and elevate by 25°.

(**Above**) A *Sturm-Infanteriegeschütz* 33B on the advance. These vehicles were almost completely wiped out during the Battle of Stalingrad. However, during the remainder of the war they formed what was known as the *Sturm-Infanteriegeschütz-Batterie/Panzer-Regiment* 201 (also known as 9.*Kompanie/Panzer-Regiment* 201). The last strength report lists five remaining in September 1944.

(**Opposite, above**) A crew can be seen here with their *Hummel* outside a workshop. During early 1944, the *Hummel* went through some modifications that included a redesign of the front glacis plate sections, with a new driver's compartment built across the width of the hull. More space was also made for the radio-operator.

(**Opposite, below**) A crew with their *Sturmpanzer* inside Warsaw in August 1944. This vehicle belonged to *Sturmpanzer-Kompanie zbV.* 218 that was raised in August 1944. It was sent to the Polish capital where it was attached to *Panzer Abteilung (Fkl)* 302. Following the Warsaw Uprising the company remained on the Eastern Front until the unit was eventually destroyed in East Prussia in 1945.

(**Opposite, above**) A *Hummel* displaying a full summer camouflage scheme during operations on the Eastern Front. The light framework in front of the driver's position was used to assist the driver in lining up the vehicle for firing.

(**Opposite, below**) A *Hummel* clearly displaying the open driver's hatch. By 1944, the *Hummel* was able to give the Panzer divisions the much heavier punch they needed when mounting counter-attacks. However, like all the vehicles in the German arsenal there were never enough to meet the ever-increasing demand for this type of weapon.

(**Above**) Two *Hummels* halted along the side of the road to allow support traffic and other armour to pass.

(**Opposite, above**) A battery of *Wespes* during a fire mission in Poland in 1944. The bulk of the *Wespes* used during the war were deployed on the Eastern Front. However, by the summer of 1944, some *Abteilungen* were rushed to the Western Front in Normandy as reinforcements.

(**Opposite, below**) A *Sturmpanzer Stupa* passes a stationary Tiger tank belonging to the *Schwere-Panzer-Abteilung 508* near Nettuno in Italy in 1944.

(**Above**) Two *Sturmpanzers* can be seen here stationary inside an Italian town during operations in 1944. These two vehicles were part of *Sturmpanzer-Abteilung 216*. This fully-independent battalion had been transferred to Italy in early February with twenty-eight vehicles to participate in the planned counter-attack against the Allied beachhead, *Unternehmen Fischfang*. It remained in operations in Italy until the end of the war.

A column of *Hummels* belonging to the *Leibstandarte Waffen-SS* advances along a dirt road.

Three photographs showing *Hummels* loaded onto special flatbed railway cars destined for another part of the Eastern Front. In order for these transport wagons to be moved by train, special loading platforms had been constructed. This allowed loads to be entrained and detrained quickly.

A photograph taken at the moment that a battery of *Wespes* began a fire mission on the Eastern Front in August 1944. Note a number of the crew members plugging their ears as the 10.5cm projectile is fired, and the red and white aiming stake poles stowed beneath the drop tailgate. These were used forward of the gun in order to provide the gunners with an azimuth reference point for firing.

Two photographs showing the 15cm sFH.13/1(Sf) *auf GW Lorraine Schlepper (f)* in a field in France. For operations in northern France, these vehicles belonged to the 21st Panzer Division and were distributed between *Panzer-Artillerie-Regiment* 155, *Kampfgruppe Rauch Panzergrenadier-Regiment* 192, *Kampfgruppe Luck Panzergrenadier-Regiment* 125 and *1.Panzergrenadier-Abteilung (SPW)*. (BA/Bender)

Field Marshal Erwin Rommel can be seen here visiting the 21st Panzer Division in Normandy in the summer of 1944. Note that parked near some trees is a 15cm *sFH 13/1 (Sf) auf GW Lorraine Schlepper (f)*. *(BA/Bender)*

Three photographs showing an abandoned *Sturmpanzer* belonging to Stu.Pz.Abt.216 in Rome in the summer of 1944. Part-netting for camouflage can clearly be seen. The vehicle also has a coating of Zimmerit anti-magnetic mine paste over its dark yellow base paint. Olive green and red-brown camouflage paint would also have been applied.

A *Sturmpanzer* at a workshop again displaying its Zimmerit anti-magnetic mine paste application with a small *Balken-kreuz* and a tactical number '13' painted in white. Note the canvas sheeting covering the fighting compartment.

An interesting photograph showing two *Sturmpanzers* that are part of an unidentified *Sturmpanzer-Abteilung* in 1944. This is more than likely at a home station prior to departure for the Eastern Front. Both vehicles would have been painted in dark yellow.

The crew of a *Grille Ausf.*K posing for the camera in front of their self-propelled vehicle. This *Grille* was based on the *Ausf.*M chassis, which was specifically designed for self-propelled mounts. The engine was relocated to the centre of the vehicle, allowing the 15cm sIG.33 gun to be mounted at the rear. The crew's fighting compartment is taller and smaller than on the previous variant.

Two *Grille Ausf.*H variants seen on the Eastern Front. This was the early model and can be identified by its fighting compartment and the rear engine. The superstructure, built around the powerful 15cm sIG.33, gave the vehicle a low profile but left the crew very vulnerable to enemy fire. Production of these variants halted in April 1943, but there were some of them still operating months later in 1944.

Some *Hummel* crew members seen posing for the camera. The *Hummel* is painted in dark yellow. During the last months of 1944, armoured supply became so critical that lots of vehicles were seen fighting on the battlefield in overall dark yellow colouring.

An interesting photograph showing a *Hummel* crewman loading 15cm sFH.18/1 L/30 shells onto the rear of the vehicle's fighting compartment during winter operations on the Eastern Front.

A *Hummel* can be seen here halted next to a *Sturmgeschütz* III on the Eastern Front.

A Waffen-SS *Wespe* crew are preparing their vehicle for a fire mission. For firing there was storage for thirty-two rounds of high-explosive armour-piercing ammunition that had an effective range of 8,400 metres. Inside the fighting compartment were a FuG Spr f-USW radio transmitter and receiver. (NARA)

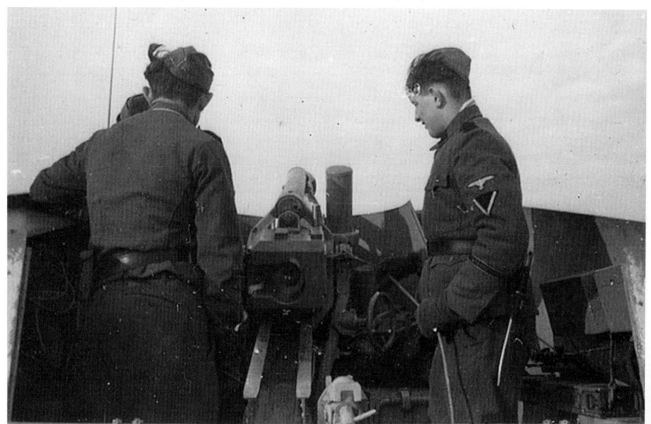

Two photographs showing *Wespes* knocked out of action in the snow. In spite of their success on the battlefield, the vehicle was prone to a number of mechanical problems including an under-powered engine that was often unable to climb steep gradients without overheating. Brakes were also an issue, including the brake linings as well.

Losses of the *Hummel* were high, especially during the last year of the war. In this photographs a *Hummel* has been almost completely destroyed by what appears to have been ammunition detonated after a hit. Note the white letter 'D' painted on the side and the sword bearing a ghost emblem. This signifies that this vehicle belonged to the 11th Panzer Division that was known as the 'Ghost Division'.

A captured *Hummel*, among other German armoured fighting vehicles, can be seen here in 1945.

Vehicle Specifications

15cm sIG.33 'Bison'

Dimensions	7.17m × 2.97m × 2.81m (23ft 5in × 9ft 7in × 9ft 2in)
Total weight (battle-ready)	23 tonnes (24.25 tons)
Crew	6 (commander, driver, 4 × gun crew)
Propulsion	12-cylinder water-cooled Maybach HL 120 TRM 11.9-litre petrol engine, 265hp at 2,600rpm
Fuel capacity	600 litres
Top speed	42km/h (26mph)
Operational range (road)	215km (133 miles)
Armament	15cm (5.9in) sFH.18/1 L/30 howitzer with 18 rounds 7.96mm (0.31in) MG 34 machine gun
Armour	Front, 30mm (1.18in); sides, 20mm (0.79in); rear, 20mm (0.79in); Superstructure front, 10mm (0.39in); sides, 10mm (0.39in)
Total production	705

Wespe

Dimensions	4.81m × 2.28m × 2.3m (15ft 9in × 7ft 6in × 7ft 7in)
Total weight (battle-ready)	11 tonnes
Crew	5 (commander, gunner, loader, driver, radio-operator)
Propulsion	Maybach HL 62 TR 140hp at 3,000rpm
Speed (road/off-road)	40km/h (25mph), 20km/h (12.5mph)
Range (road/off-road)	140km (87 miles), 95km (59 miles)
Primary armament	10.5cm leFH.18/2
Secondary armament	One 7.92mm MG 34 machine gun
Elevation	–5° to +42°
Armour	5mm (0.2in) to 30mm (1.2in)

Sturmpanzer IV Brummbär

Dimensions	5.9m × 2.8m × 2.52m (19ft 5in × 9ft 5in × 8ft 3in)
Total weight (battle-ready)	28.2 tons (62,170lb)

Armament	15cm (5.9in) StuH 43 L/12 (Series 1), StuH 43/1 L/12 (Series 2–4) (38 rounds) 7.92mm *Maschinengewehr* 34 (external machine gun)
Armour	10mm to 100mm (0.39in to 3.93in)
Crew	4 to 5 (commander, driver, gunner, 1/2 loaders)
Propulsion	Maybach HL120TRM V-12 water-cooled, gasoline 300bhp (221kW)
Speed	40 km/h (25mph) road, 24km/h (15mph) off-road
Suspension	Leaf springs
Range	210km (130 miles)
Total production	Approx. 316

Lorraine Schlepper (f)

Dimensions	4.95m × 2.1m × 2.05m (16ft 2in × 6ft 9in × 6ft 7in)
Total weight (battle-ready)	7.7 tonnes
Crew	4 (commander, gunner, loader, driver)
Propulsion	Delahaye-type 135, 70hp at 2,800rpm
Speed	35km/h (22mph), 8km/h (5mph) (cross-country)
Operational range	120km (74.5 miles), 75km (46.5 miles) (cross-country)
Primary armament	10.5cm (4.1in) leFH.18
Secondary armament	7.92mm MG 34
Elevation	−20° to +20°
Traverse	25° to the right and 32° to the left
Armour	Superstructure, 10–11mm Hull, 6–12mm

Grille (38t)

Dimensions	4.95m × 2.15m × 2.47m (16ft 2in × 7ft 1in × 8ft 10in)
Total weight (battle-ready)	11.5 tonnes
Crew	4 (commander, gunner, loader, driver)
Propulsion	Praga AC 6-cylinder petrol, 147hp
Speed	35km/h (22mph), 8km/h (5mph) (cross-country)
Operational range	190km (118 miles) (cross-country)
Primary armament	15cm (5.9in) sIG.33 howitzer, 15 rounds
Secondary armament	7.92mm MG 34
Armour	Superstructure, 10–11mm Hull, 6–12mm

Camouflage and Zimmerit

In June 1941, when the Germans invaded Russia, virtually all self-propelled armour along with the Panzers was painted in dark grey. For the first four months of Operation BARBAROSSA the vehicles in their overall dark grey camouflage scheme blended in well with the local terrain. However, with the drastic onset of winter and the first snow showers at the end of October 1941, the crews would soon be filled with anxiety as their vehicles were not camouflaged for winter warfare. With the worrying prospect of fighting in Russia in the snow, the *Wehrmacht* reluctantly issued washable white winter camouflage paint in November 1941. The paint was specially designed to be thinned with water and applied to all vehicles and equipment where snow was on the ground. This new winter whitewash paint could easily be washed off by the crews in the spring, thereby exposing the dark grey base colour. Unfortunately for the crews, the order came too late and the distribution to the front lines was delayed by weeks. Consequently, the crews had to improvise and find various crude substitutes with which to camouflage their vehicles. This included some hastily applying a rough coat of lime whitewash to their vehicles, while others used lumps of chalk, white cloth strips and sheets, and even hand-packed snow in a drastic attempt to conceal the most conspicuous dark grey parts. Other vehicles, however, roamed the white arctic wilderness with no camouflage at all.

Following the harsh winter of 1941, spring of 1942 saw the return of the dark grey base colour on all the vehicles. It was during this period that a number of vehicles saw the return of pre-war dark brown and dark green camouflage schemes. Crews had learned from the previous year that the lessons of camouflage and survival were paramount for these young men. For this reason many crews had begun utilizing and adding to their camouflage schemes by finding various substitutes and applying them to the surface of the vehicles. This included the widespread use of foliage and bundles of grass and hay. This was a particularly effective method and was often used to break up the distinctive shapes and allow them to blend into the local terrain. Mud was also used as an effective form of camouflage, but was never universally appreciated by the crews.

For the first time in southern Russia, in the Crimea and the Caucasus where the summer weather was similar to that of North Africa, many vehicles were given an application of tropical camouflage, with the widespread use of sand colour schemes almost identical to those used in the *Afrika-Korps*. In southern Russia in the summer the terrain was very similar to that of a desert and for that reason the vehicles were completed in the tropical colours of yellow-brown RAL 8000, grey-green RAL 7008 or just brown RAL 8017.

By 1943, olive green was being used on vehicles, weapons and large pieces of equipment. A red-brown colour RAL 8012 also had been introduced at the same time. These two colours, along with a new colour base of dark yellow RAL 7028, were issued to crews in the form of a highly-concentrated paste. The paste arrived in 2kg and 20kg cans, and units were ordered to apply these cans of coloured paste over the entire surface of the vehicles. The paste was specially adapted so that it could be thinned with water or even fuel, and could be applied by spray, a brush or a mop.

The dark yellow paste was issued primarily to cover unwanted colours or areas of the camouflage schemes, especially during changes in seasons. These new variations of colours gave the crews the widest possible choice of schemes so as to blend in as much as possible with the local terrain. The pastes were also used to colour all canvas tops and tarpaulins on the vehicles.

The new three-colour paint scheme worked very well on the front lines and allowed each unit maximum advantage depending on the surrounding conditions. However, within months there were frequent problems with supply. Support vehicles carrying the new paste had to travel so far to various scattered units, even from railheads, that frequently Panzer units never received any new application of camouflage schemes. Another problem was due to the fact that many Panzer units were already heavily embroiled in bitter fighting and had neither the vehicles to spare nor the manpower to pull them out of the line for a repaint. Even rear-area ordnance workshops were returning vehicles to action at such a rate that they only managed to replace parts and then send them back to the front without repainting. A great many vehicles never received any paste colours at all, and those that fought on remained in dark yellow, with crews sometimes adapting and enhancing the scheme with the application of foliage and mud.

However, of all the failings, the greatest of them all was actually the paints themselves. These proved to be unstable when mixed with water, and even the slightest downpour of rain could cause these new colours to run or wash off the vehicles. Even fuel, which was used to give the paste a durable finish, was at such a premium during the latter stages of the war that units were compelled to use water, waste oil and mixtures of other paints. All this caused immense variation in the appearance of the paint schemes and as a consequence there were unusual colours such as brick-red, chocolate-brown and light green. In spite of these variations in colour and the fact that there had become little standardization in the camouflage schemes, occasionally there were complete units that appeared on the front lines properly painted and marked, but this was often a rare occurrence, especially by 1944.

Throughout 1944, a further drain on German supplies and resources caused considerable disruption to materials. The paint system on the vehicles was just one of many hundreds of deprivations that were inflicted on the already badly depleted armoured units. During the last months of 1944, armoured supply became critical and lots of vehicles were seen in overall dark yellow colouring.

By this time almost all the new vehicles that had left the last remaining factories for the front lines were in their base colour of dark yellow. They never received any further camouflage treatment, other than being covered with foliage.

The use of foliage during the last year of the war was extensive. Most vehicles and a large range of weapons had foliage attached to break up their distinctive shapes. The Germans were masters in the art of camouflaging their vehicles with branches from trees, grass and hay. In fact, some vehicles carried so much foliage that it was sometimes difficult to determine what types of vehicle they were or what camouflage scheme they had. In the last furious year of the war, foliage had become more important than colours.

Notes